# GOD'S
## PROTECTION IN THE
## MIDST OF DANGER

# GOD'S
# PROTECTION IN THE
# MIDST OF DANGER

BY

ROGER BERNARD ANDERSON, SR

ARPress
ILLUMINATING IDEAS
EMPOWERING VOICES

**ARPress**
45 Dan Road Suite 5
Canton MA 02021

Hotline:      1(888) 821-0229
Fax:          1(508) 545-7580

Ordering Information:

Quantity sales. Special discounts are available on quantity purchases by corporations, associations, and others. For details, contact the publisher at the address above.

Printed in the United States of America.

ISBN-13:      Paperback      979-8-89330-979-9
              eBook          979-8-89330-980-5
              Hardback       979-8-89330-981-2

Library of Congress Control Number: 2024902593

# Table of Contents

# Acknowledgements

I would like to thank my heavenly Father for this wonderful opportunity He has granted me to write this novel. I am forever grateful for my loving, inspiring, and wonderful wife Jennifer Leigh Anderson, who was more than enough support for me in doing so. She was instrumental in helping me to put my story on paper so that others could be inspired. To my children and all my family and friends who not only supported me but prayed for me and all the other soldier's safety while being deployed in support of Operation Iraqi Freedom. I would like to send a special thank you to my beloved Pastor, Elder Eugene Fields who departed this world in December of 2003, to be with the Lord while I was still deployed in Iraq. Thanks to my mother Betty J. Anderson, my siblings, and Sis. Juanita Barker for being so supportive and faithful in their prayers. I want to thank the Lord also for the saints all over the world that was praying relentless for us day and night, thanks for your faithfulness. Not to forget my brothers in the Lord Elder Richard Murphy, Elder Leon Dedrick, and Bro. Jesse Coates who was also my battle buddy who never said a word at night when I was using my flashlight as light to do my writing. Also, to everyone else who was supporting me and praying for me and the other soldiers while we were stationed in the country of Iraq Thanks again. Without the letters and care packages our journey would have been more difficult, but to God be the glory for all he has done, thank you Lord and thank you everybody!

ALL THE GLORY BELONGS TO THE LORD

# Preface

If you believe in God, You already know that you are covered under His blood. We are now faced with decisions and obstacles as we enter into this new world era. We know that things have moved to a different realm, and they are rapidly changing on the face of this earth. As children of God we have to listen to Him and feel the urge to seek Him more as we crave after His righteousness.

"If my people, which are called by My name, shall humble themselves, and pray and seek My face, and turn from their wicked ways; then will I hear from heaven, and will forgive their sin, and will heal their land." 2 Chronicles 7:14, (kjv)It is time to seek God like never before.

It's time for us to run to the altar and fall down and ask God to help us praise him more and teach us to be more obedient at doing his will. In church today, many are playing church; ask God to give you a heart that longs after His will.

As I began to write this book, I realized that I could only be lead by God to outline the chapters he has given to 2me to be shared with you. Bear in mind that what is said for your reading is moved upon me by the Holy Spirit. As you continue to read on in this book, you will see that this is a work and move of the Spirit of God.

This novel has been in the making, but I just had to wait on my guidance from the Lord. The road of how I got here, has been difficult; sometimes painful, not fair, evil, and trying so I know it will be a spiritual inspiration as the writing begins to unfold. The church, as we have known it, is not the same. If we just stand back and take a look we can see before even realizing it; we have fallen into error, even while we have continued to do good things for God. We have tripped, stumbled, and fallen in doing what God requires of us. Now He is making the call for us to get back up and get on track. The words of the Apostle Paul states, "When I thought to do good, evil was always present." This reminds me that I must be true and obedient and always seeking the Lord for guidance.

"For a just man falleth seven times, and riseth up again: but the wicked shall fall into mischief." Proverbs 24:16 (kjv)

**With God we have to make things personal, for it is possible to be close to Christ, yet so far from the life He offers.** As I studied on His original twelve apostles, I found that this was true. Even in that inner circle there was one, probably the most trusted member of the group, who never really had the kind of personal connection with Christ that

we are talking about. Judas knew a lot about Jesus and he knew The Teacher's habits well enough to lead Jesus' enemies to a garden meeting place. He knew Christ well 3enough to betray himwith a kiss of greeting, but Judas didn't know Jesus as his Savior and Lord. Trusted though he was, the keeper of the money, Judas never had the kind of personal, Christ-centered relationship with God that is available to us today.

**Knowing Christ died, that's history. Believing He died for me, that's salvation.** A personal relationship with God begins with an event Jesus called a new birth (John 3:3). When we are born spiritually into God's family, we become His children and members of His spiritual kingdom. To begin this personal relationship, and to know that you are protected; you need to take these following steps.

**1. Admit your need : Know that we came into this world physically alive, but spiritually dead; missing out on the quality of Life for which God made us.**

**2. Realize what God has done for you: God loved us enough to send His own Son into this world to rescue us from the devastating effects of our sins. (John 1:1-14; 3:16)**

**3. Personally believe and receive God's gift: We know that no one is saved by trying to be good. We are saved by trusting in Christ."For by grace are ye saved through faith; and that not of yourselves: it is the gift of God: not of works, lest any man should boast." Ephesians 2:8-9 (kjv**

# Poem # 1

## (In The Potter's Hand)

*When we think of the Potter*
*What do we see,*
*Our Lord and Savior*
*Shaping you and me.*

*Have thine own way, Lord! Have thine own way*
*Thou are the potter, I am the clay;*
*Mold me and make me after thy will,*
*While I am waiting, yielded and still.*

*What I couldn't do*
*My great potter could,*
*I only needed to be cooperative clay*
*So Christ could do the heavenly will.*

*When we think of the potter*
*Receiving our every prayer,*
*We can delight in words and praise him everywhere*
*Knowing that he is always there.*

*Though I know not what awaits me*
*What the future has in store,*
*Yet I know that God is faithful*
*For I've proved him oft before.*

*Forgive me, O Lord, for all of my sins,*
*Please make my heart pure and cleanse me within;*
*To you I confess, my ways have been wrong;*
*Restore now my joy and fill me with a song.*

*In Jesus name our prayer we praise,*
*Through the potter's guiding hand has blessed our days;*
*And may we, Lord, in glory fear*
*Serve you throughout this new year.*

*Today this vessel is far from finished*
*And there is a lot more that God can do,*
*So I challenge you my sisters and brothers to enjoy the new*
*Sit back and see what the great Potter can do for you.*

*God can take a lowly vessel*
*Shape it with His mighty hand,*
*Fill it with a matchless treasure*
*And make it serve a purpose grand.*

# *Introduction*
## *How It All Began*

An all of a sudden change in your life is both challenging and uncomfortable. You will never know peace until you have peace with God, peace that comes from knowing and alking with God. In doing so, there are several things that affects your walk with God. First, your personal relationship with God, your call from God, your devotional life, your message, your social concern, your relationship with your Christian friends, and your evangelism.

The other disciples never dreamed that in his heart Judas had never come into a real relationship with Jesus Christ. Having this relationship is what the prophet Jeremiah meant when he wrote, " His words are in mine heart as a burning fire shut up in my bones." Do you sense this burning within your bones? Have you been called by God to be in the place where you are? Today many seminary students are growing up and going into the ministry as a profession but has never been called by God.

As my sisters and brothers were growing up my mother always kept us submissive to her and other elderly people. I always knew that while growing up, times will get tough and the route will grow harder to travel. As a young kid, I knew that God had something special for me in this life and the one to come. There was always an urge for me to do more spiritual; in order for me to achieve any goals that were set before me. What was God doing in my life? I was too young to understand; but it was the plan He had already set for me to follow.

As time passed and I grew to become a man, things began to change. As time passed and I grew to become a man, things began to change. In 1996, the Lord was ushering me into the plan he had set before me minister his word. In 1996, the Lord was ushering me into the plan he had set before me to minister his word. In 1997, He placed His anointing upon me so heavily that I couldn't walk away from His call to be a mouth piece to speak His word. The Lord helped me to start my ministry at the State Cattle Ranch in Lock , a small rural area in the state of Alabama. As we would go down on the first Sunday of each month, my pastor, Elder Eugene Fields, would just sit back and allow one of his ministers to speak to the inmates. It was so exciting to see the young men coming to Christ and giving their life to Him. It was a blessing for me because it helped me to work out my fear of being around inmates. I used to fear them because I labeled them as murderers, when most of them were drug pushers or sex offenders. Nevertheless, I had to learn that God's love didn't just reach me and stop, it longed for all who seek him. If it was a need that needed to be met, these guys definitely needed a move of God in their life. As God began to flourish my ministry and increase my faith in Him, that's when the enemy stepped in and tried to side swipe me and knock me off track and out of God's plan. When things got tough it was like opening a bag of chips from one end and the opposite end already open. The devil started attacking my mind because that is his favorite spot to begin with. He plays with your thoughts and emotions to get your mind off the Lord.

Once he has attacked the mind, he can steer you the way he wants to. With the devil, it's like driving a car. Once you are in control of the car you can go; and take it where you want. Once he began dealing with your mind, he had access to your whole life because you allowed him to control you. He start attacking everything that he could, first the marriage, then the children, and then the love for God. When you are at this point, you have no where else to turn but to God. No matter how much your pride and ego won't let you. This is the time for you to realize that the God you serve is far more powerful than anyne else and any circumstance. At this point you start telling yourself that, greater is He that is in me, than He that is in the world. Once you received this in your spirit and started believing God, it was then that my life started to get back on track.

When I open my heart to receive God's word; I heardHis word minister to my spirit.

"And when he putteth forth his own sheep, he goeth before them, and the sheep will follow him: for they know his voice. And a stranger will they not follow, but will flee from him: for they know not the voice of strangers." St. John 10:4- (kjv)Now the work that God has for me can be put into action, but I had to remain aware that the devil, my enemy, is still on the prawl. Although I'm ready to surrender my all to

God, Satan doesn't like the fact that he has lost another soul to God. This is what makes me say, I will bless the Lord at all times and His praises will continuously be in my mouth. Serve the Lord, it's worth having Him in your life. He will reshape and renew your body, mind, and soul; remember He is the potter and you are the clay.

## TO GOD BE THE GLORY!

# Poem #2
## (It Is Time To Pray)

*When people face trials*
*They turn to prayer as the last resort,*
*But wouldn't it be ashame*
*When God looks and says depart.*

*Instead of prayer being a last resort*
*It should be the first thing we do,*
*The Lord will answer your prayers*
*If you let him come to you.*

*Any hour he is there*
*Or when helping others,*
*To bear their heavy cares*
*It's the proper time for prayer.*

*One life to live for Christ my Lord*
*One life to do my part,*
*One life in which to give my all*
*With fervency of my heart.*

*At times our fears may loom so large*
*We pray for proof that God is near,*
*It's then our father says to us*
*Have faith, my child, and do not fear.*

*O help me, Lord, to show respect*
*To always pray and honor you, the best*
*That I may bring you the highest praise*
*In everything I do and say.*

*The comfort God has given us*
*He wants us now to share,*

*With others who are suffering*
*And caught in life's despair.*

*Trying to bring God's love and kindness*
*Into someone's life today,*
*Is getting more complex*
*Because we don't take the time to pray*

# Chapter One

## What We Should Do In This Time?

In today's society, we are faced with many challenges and calamities that bear down on us day after day. With the killing and violence that we have in our streets, this is the question you hear a lot. What we should do in this time? What are we going to do as parents to stop the unnecessary killing? What are we going to do about our international problems that links us throughout the world? I would recommend taking a lesson from a wise builder from the Bible days.

"The earth also was corrupt before God, and the earth was filled with violence. And God looked upon the earth, and behold, it was corrupt; for all the flesh had corrupted His way upon the earth." Genesis 6:11-12 (kjv)12Roger Bernard Anderson, Sr.With these things taken place, we must understand that if something needed to be done then surely it needs to take place today. The question at hand is who would be God's vessel to be used in this age. Just as God instructed Noah to build himself an ark to protect himself from the destruction to come, we are to build us an ark of protection for ourselves to keep us safe from this wicked and untoward generation.

**Building yourself an ark** `

When you build anything that needs to stand the test of time, it needs to be built on a true and solid foundation. Again, just as God instructed Noah to build himself an ark he is definitely telling us we need to adapt this same method and build us one. We need to build this ark not of wood, but of the word of God. One must realize that what you know from the word of God can and will save your life. If you build yourself up in the word of God and trust that He will keep you in the midst of danger, you can live in this crazy world with all of its danger and still feel secure and free. You don't have to be frightened by the things that are happening around you because even in the worst of times, God has proven he has the wonderful ability to deliver His people from danger.

## Expect the unexpected

While you are in this world, you don't know what to do or expect, but now that you have become a child of God you can expect the unexpected, as well as, the impossible. With God, there are lots of benefits; some of which you may not know of. To sum up what I am saying in just one word, I would say salvation is soundness in every area of your life. It includes all the benefits from God, healing for your body, 13peace for your mind, righteousness for your spirit, physical and spiritual protection, prosperity and financial blessing.

"Blessed be the Lord, who daily loadeth us with benefits, even the God of our salvation. Selah. He that is our God is the God of salvation; and unto God the Lord belong the issues from death." Psalm 68:19-20 (kjv)

At this point, I know some of you may be wondering why these things are not happening for me, but you must know that they don't just happen automatically; because they don't come automatically. They are manifested in your life only as you begin to trust God for them specifically. To explain further of what I'm talking about. When God promised, "that if thou shalt confess with thy mouth the Lord Jesus, and shalt believe in thine heart that God raised Him from the dead, thou shalt be saved." Romans 10:9

In other words, once you have repented and confessed your sins before God and received his Holy Spirit, you are a new creature. You are born again from this wicked world and you have just experienced what it is like to come out of spiritual darkness and into the marvelous light of Jesus Christ. (Col. 1:13) Now just because you have been forgiven of your sins, you are still vulnerable to sickness of this world and yes, God said that He would heal all matter of sickness, but you must except first that you have it and then give it to him to work it out and deliver you. This is why it's so important for you to know God's protection in the midst of danger. You receive blessings by faith and faith comes by hearing the word, so it's true, you can't have faith for something you don't know about.

## Let's Pray Together

### Heavenly Father,

I know that things are changing and heading in all directions, so right now we need you more than ever. We want to thank you for your grace and mercy you have given to us. God we want to cast all our cares upon you so that we can be free in handling your business. At this moment God we need you to breathe your breath of anointing on us so that we can withstand the wiles of the enemy. Father, although, life choices presses us daily we need you to survive. We don't know the answer to all the problems nor can we figure them all out, but Lord I pray that you give us strength to overcome our daily obstacles and learn to trust you more. Moreover we need your guidance to help us make the best choice and give the best answer to whatever situation or problem we may face. In times like these people turn to everything else but you Lord, so as life problems unfold give us the voice to say what needs to be said.

And Lord lead us in the right direction and give us open minds and hearts to hear Your Word and to allow the Holy Spirit to teach us Your purposes and truth. We pray this in the name of Jesus, our Wisdom and our Strength. Amen.

## Poem # 3
### ( The Call To War )

*The call to war is not an everyday call*
*You must be prepared mentally, physically, and all,*
*It will change your mind, your heart, and thought process*
*Because the call to war is a rapid progress.*

*Your call to duty is to serve your country*
*With all the excitement, attitudes, and all,*
*Just remember how important your call is*
*Because war is not an everyday call.*

*Both men and women may loose their lives*
*In the line of fire that we call war,*
*But if you train hard to fight and win*
*Loosing your life, some may say is a just cause.*

*No one planned to put their lives on hold*
*But there was no hope,*
*The UN must of felt like kids*
*When the boss didn't honor their vote.*

*Sometimes being in high positions you pay the price*
*No one listens most of the time and sometimes not at all,*
*Just remember that war is not an everyday call.*

*We've came, we've fought, and we've won*
*How exciting this must have been,*
*But before we all journey back home*
*We must be certain it's not the end.*

*It's time to go home and be with our family and friends*
*The talk of war I wouldn't do again,*
*Although lives have been lost, we prayed for you all*
*We just had to honor this unforgettable call.*

# Chapter Two

## Dealing With The Separation

To be absent from your family is lonely, stressful, painful and boring. Being separated from anything or anyone you love is very painful, especially when you are not sure when or if you are coming back. This happened to me and my fellow soldiers of the 1166th Military Police Company from Greensboro and Thomasville, Alabama on February 7, 2003; when we were activated to serve in the middle east in Support of Operation Iraqi Freedom. When the orders came down, no one knew what to expect nor what to do, it left everyone silent. Restless but , we were in dying need of a word from the Lord. We could hear the whispering of God saying, "He that dwelleth in the secret place of the most high shall abide under the shadow of the almighty. Psalms 91:1." This was a word that I needed to hear to share it with some of the other soldiers to ensure them that everything is sure to be alright. For some of us, it was the first time that we had left our loved ones for more than a two week duty, once a year, but for others they were involved in Desert Storm /Shield in 1991. After listening at the voice of God, telling me, "you must abide and trust in me if you want to make it." God assures us that in order for us to enjoy His protection, we must abide in Him. To abide, which means to dwell in, it is a word that implies not a temporary situation but a permanent dwelling place, the place where you make your home. How can we become an abider? This question is answered in John 15:7, Jesus said, "If ye abide in me, and my words abide in you, ye shall ask what ye will, and it shall be done unto you."

God's word is truth and that truth is alive in your heart, and it is the truth that you act on everyday. This truth doesn't come from simply reading a scripture once, shouting hallelujah, and going on pretending. It comes from knowing the word so well that it comes to you thinking instantly in a crisis situation. The truth comes alive in you when you think about it, meditate on it and apply it to your life, so at the moment of danger, the word of God is your first thought. I had a teacher from the high school in which I graduated, asked that I read Psalm 91 as my daily devotion, but I had no idea why, but I thank God for her, Mrs. Gould. I pondered over this text for a very long time, then it opened my eyes; that to be an abider you needed to be consistent. ( Stay in the word of God read daily, and recieve the 91st Psalm into your mind daily until it is engrafted into your heart.

## The 91st Book of Psalms

*1. He that dwelleth in the secret place of the most High shall abide under the shadow of the Almighty.*
*2. I will say of the Lord, He is my refuge and my fortress: my God; in him will I trust.*
*3. Surely he shall deliver thee from the snare of the fowler, and from the noisome pestilence.*
*4. He shall cover thee with his feathers, and under his wings shalt thou trust: his truth shall be thy shield and buckler.*
*5. Thou shalt not be afraid for the terror by night; nor the arrow that flieth by day;*
*6. Nor for the pestilence that walketh in darkness; nor for the estruction that wasteth at noonday.*
*7. A thousand shall fall at thy side, and ten thousand at thy right hand; but it shall not come nigh thee.*
*8. Only with thine eyes shalt thy behold and see the reward or the wicked.*
*9. Because thou hast made the Lord, which is my refuge, even the most High, thy habitation;*
*10. There shall no evil befall thee, neither shall any plague come nigh thy dwelling.*
*11. For he shall give his angels charge over thee, to keep thee in all thy ways.*
*12. They shall bear thee up in their hands, lest thou dash thy foot against a stone.*

*13. Thou shalt tread upon a lion and adder: the young lion and the dragon shalt trample under feet.*
*14. Because he hath set his love upon me, therefore will I deliver him: I will set him on high, because he hath known my name.*
*15. He shall call upon me, and I will answer him: I will be with him in trouble; I will deliver him, and honor him.*
*16. With long life will I satisfy him, and shew him my salvation*

Separation from family, friends, and your country is not an easy pill to swallow. During this time of war, separation causes many unusual things to happen and lots of enemies are made. But, one thing I can say is thank you God we are living in the days of His grace and mercy and it's never to late to call upon the Lord. If you haven't been abiding in the word, it's going to be difficult for you to call on Him with faith when disappointments and calamities come. Proverbs 1:33 states, "But whosoever hearken unto me shall dwell safely, and shall be quiet from fear of evil." Studying God's word on a daily basis, keeps us not only safe, but honest with Him at all times. This and this alone assures us that God's protection in the midst of danger is relevant to all. "God is our refuge and strength, a very present help in trouble. Therefore, we will not fear, though the earth be removed, and though the mountains be carried into the midst of the sea." Proverbs 46:1-2 states,"God is just, and loyal to all and He is sure to deliver on time." Remember that when Jesus was on His journey preaching and teaching to His disciples He oftentimes withdrew himself to pray. At some point and time we would wonder why he did / what he did / the way he did it. He was doing no more than showing us that there may be times when we will either be separated or just have withdrawn ourselves from others. Jesus was letting us know that being separated from others is not all that bad, but sometimes it is for the good. As saints of God we have to constantly tell ourselves we are the clay and the Lord is The Potter and He can do with us what He likes, because we are the work of His hands. Sometimes the separation can happen instantly and you have to separate yourself immediately to pray. Withdrawing yourself can be done without leaving the presence of the person or that place.

If you ever take a clay pottery class one lesson that you will learn very quickly, is no project will be successful unless the clay was precisely centered on the spinning wheel before you begin to work with it. If you are not careful cups and bowls that looked promising will collapsed if the ball of clay is off center. One thing to keep in mind is that you will have to concentrate hard and use some supernatural strength to hold the clay firmly in your hands when the wheel began spinning. So as you try to feel the center of the wheel you may have to close your eyes because what looked like the center could be deceiving . Once you find the center, you could mold the clay into useful and sometimes beautiful things. As you read this it should not be hard to find a parallel between this lesson and your relationship with God. If you make a deliberate effort everyday to make God the center of your life, your life can be useful and reflect the beauty of God's love. If you are focus and have a heart desire to obey God, you will become a useful vessel. The prophet Jeremiah stated " Ask where the good way is, and walk in it, and you will find rest for your soul."

( As I sit and think about when I was smaller in grade school how we would ride bicycles and I would ride my brother, we would do it joyfully because he knew deep down that as his older brother) I would take care of him. It didn't matter how fast, or how far we went he was still trusting in me for safety. Just as my brother felt secure with me steering and pedaling the bicycle, we should trust God with our lives. I could see the road ahead and steered a course that would get us where we were going, and God sees our future and knows our path. God knows the way we should go; we can rely on God to plot our route and we would be sure to stay the course. We can feel secure if we let God be our guide and protector. As my brother trusted me on our routes, we can trust our Heavenly Father for each day's journey. Dealing with the separation is not as hard as we think "when we, make our petition known to God" and he promise to take care of them and gives us rest. The separation from family, friends, and my country revealed my faith, my strength, and my relationship with God. It provided me with an x-ray of my body, mind, and spirit. During this separation my relationship with my Heavenly Father grew stronger and it was then that I sensed the understanding of King David in the book of Psalm when he stated: (In the fullness of God there is Joy). Spiritually I was elevated in Christ from being separated from my family, friends, and my country. I say to you my sisters and brothers when you are in a foreign land whether spiritual or physical trust God and He will increase your faith. Therefore, you will be able to speak to a mountain and say mountain be moved and believe it will be done.

## Let's Pray Together

**Heavenly Father,**

We know that you are a God of purpose, and your purpose is eternal. Father you have said, " Many are the plans in a man's heart, but it is the Lord's purpose that prevails" (Proverbs 19:21). We ask you to establish whatever is from You and whatever is in line with your purpose and cause to fade away whatever is not from you. It is times like these that shows who has total dependency on the Lord. Today Lord we honor you as our Creator and as our loving heavenly Father. Lord we affirm that it is you who work in us to will and to act according to Your good purpose. Renew our minds that we may understand Your ways and Your plans more fully. We pray this in the name of Jesus, who is our Way, Truth, and Life. Amen.

# Poem # 4
## ( The Test of Criticisms )

*Morning light motivates a desire*
*To reach out and help others,*
*Doing this for the Lord*
*Is a sure sign of helping your brother.*

*Am I wrong today in men eye sight*
*When I say "let's do," and you say "why do,"*
*Should we be building up or tearing down*
*The brothers and sisters that we are around.*

*Who has the right to criticize*
*When my heart desires to help,*
*Getting over this annoying problem*
*Is to make a higher step.*

*I know sometimes it makes you upset*
*But that is only your test,*
*When situations as these arrive*
*Thank God you are still able to rest.*

*When life's afflictions batter you*
*Like waves upon the sand,*
*Remember to look up to God*
*And take his outstretched hand.*

*Lord, help us to be honest*
*In all that we do and say,*
*And grant us the grace and power*
*To live for you each day.*

*Take control of our heart today*
*Keep it filled with joy and praise,*

*And gratitude for every good*
*You bestow on our days.*

*Help us to see the good and bad*
*Through our very own eyes,*
*To be sure and understand*
*That what others say or do is just to criticize*

# Chapter Three

## When Is The Need
## To Say Something?

Job states in his writing, " How painful are honest words! But what do your arguments prove? Do you mean to correct what I say, and treat the words of a despairing man as wind? You would even cast lots for the fatherless and barter away your friend. But now be so kind as to look at me. Would I lie to your face? Relent, do not be unjust; reconsider, for my integrity is at stake. Is there wickedness on my lips? Can my mouth not discern malice?" Job has not asked the Lord for anything except what will cost him nothing, but friendship and counsel. Having replied to Eliphaz, Job now addresses his complaint toward God. The Book of Job Chapter 7:1 –21

*1. "Does a man have hard service on earth? Are not his days like those of a hired man?*
*2. Like a slave longing for the evening shadows, or a hired man waiting eagerly for his wages,*
*3. So I have been allotted months of futility, and nights of misery have been assigned to me. 4. When I lie down I think, how long before I get up? The nights drags on, and I toss till dawn.*
*5. My body is clothed with worms and scabs, my skin is broken and festering. 6. My days are swifter than a weaver's shuttle, and they come to an end without hope. 7. Remember, O God that my life is but a breath; my eyes will never see happiness again.*
*8. The eye that now sees me will see me no longer; you will look for me, but I will be no more.*
*9. As a cloud vanishes and is gone, so he who goes down to the grave does not return.*
*10. He will never come to his house again; his place will know him no more.*

*11. Therefore I will not keep silent; I will speak out bitterness of my soul.*

*12. Am I the sea, or the monster of the deep, that you put me under uard?*

*13. When I think my bed will comfort me and my couch will ease my complaint,*

*14. Even then you frighten me with dreams and terrify me with visions,*

*15. So that I prefer strangling and death, rather than this body of mine.*

*16. I despise my life; I would not live forever. Let me alone; my days have no meaning.*

*17. What is man that you make so much of him, that you give him so much attention,*

*18. That you examine him every morning and test him every moment?*

*19. Will you never look away from me, or let me alone even for an instant?*

*20. If I have sinned, what have I done to you, O watcher of men? Why have you made me your*

*target? Have I become a burden to you ?*

*21. Why do you not pardon my offenses and forgive my sins? For I will soon lie down in the dust; you will search for me, but I will be no more.*"

The question, "when is the need to say something?" It arrives in one's mind when the troubles of life comes knocking at their door. When this happens, you might not hear what someone is saying, neither what God is trying to tell you. One thing we can be assure of is that He loves us no matter what or what state we may be in. In the midst of the storm, it is time for you to say what the psalmist said, "I will say of the Lord, He is my refuge and my fortress; my God, in Him will I trust." Psalms 91:2

God is a God of righteousness and a God that holds you in His love and care, both day and night; regardless of your troubles and trials. There are times when we are put in positions that we have no choice but to say that He is my Savior, My keeper, My deliverer. Not only will we make wrong decisions, but there will be times when we question ourselves, "why is life so unfair?" That's when God steps in and assures us that nothing He has created is unfair. The worldly choices we make in this life tends to lead us in directions other than where God would haveus to go. As Christians, we have to realize that everything God made is good; so no matter what we are faced with just remember His word in the book of Romans 8:28 states: "And we know that all things work together for the good to them that love God, to them who are the called according to His purpose." These words are like a soft pillow for your tired heart.

Even though situations can seem hopeless, there is still hope at the end of your rope. The cares of this life is filled with such expectations that the cost of being a disciple is at an all time low, so as children of God we need to ask Him to show us His ways and teach us his paths while leading us in His truth.

Psalm 91:3-4 (NIV) states "Surely, He will save you from the fowler's snare and from the deadly pestilence. He will cover you with his feathers, and under His wings you will find refuge; His faithfulness will be your shield and rampart." Truly there will be times when the enemydesires to sift you as wheat and break your cycle and steal your joy. Occasionally, it's helpful to spend some quiet moments looking back over our lives to review how God's love gives goodness and mercy. As being debtors to Christ, the need to say something is never, so this is what the psalmist meant when he said, surely goodness and mercy shall follow me all the days of my life and I will dwell in the house of the Lord forever. God's goodness imparts what we don't deserve. In times of pain and sorrow, our

Heavenly Father faithfully meets our needs, comforts, our hearts and gives us strength to bear our burdens. The need to say something at this point is to tell God thank you, I love you, and I worship you. Remember that when you do speak let it be with comfort, for Jesus said, "with love and kindness have I drawn you," so we are to be no different. Sharing what you know will not only bless someone else, but release them from the struggles that they have. James 5:7-8 (NIV) states: "Be patient, then, brothers, until the Lord's coming. See how the farmer waits for the land to yield it's valuable crop and how patient he is for the autumn and spring rains. You too, be patient and stand firm, because the Lord's coming is near." We have to realize that as Christians we have hope in Jesus Christ. Just as the sunflowers follows the sun on the those sunny days for the strength and support to grow, we to must trust and rely on God's word for our strength and growth. Everyday is not going to be a bushel of roses and no one has said that it would be. But one thing we can be assure of and that is, there's life in Christ. Not only us, but there are other's that are not save and want to be save, but there is no helping hands to help steer them in the right direction. As we take a look at Jesus he spent much of his time working with those who had been put aside by others; the poor, the prostitutes, the lepers, and the mentally ill. Those whom others shunned, Jesus saw as valuable children of God. He sought them out, picked them up, healed them and cleansed their souls, and lovingly restored them to useful service in God's kingdom.

In today's world, we see people everyday who appear broken, and deep down we ask ourselves when is the need to say something? Some may seem beyond repair: The homeless, the inmate, the drug addict, the greedy business executive who always wants more, and the tyrant. Jesus calls us to see beyond people's problems, to love them and restore them to useful service in God's kingdom. As we look at the prodigal son when he was slump with unfair treatment that was caused by himself, he realized that it was time to say something. When he started home, he probably felt that his situation was hopeless. He had strayed from his family and lived in a shameful, sinful manner. He did not expect to be accepted into his family again. At best, he might be welcomed as a servant, but his father threw his arms around him and welcomed him home.

No person nor any situation is hopeless. Our God is a God of hope and grace. As Jesus said, " For God all things are possible, " so don't think that when you have something to say that you should be silent, go ahead say what's needed to be said, you could help someone who is listening.

I totally agree with the scriptures that it is easier for us to see the specks in others' eyes than to see the log in our on eye. My personal devotional times gives me the opportunity to look at myself honestly. In these moments of silent reflection, I look back not only at my experiences, but also at my responses. I know that the presence of the counselor and the prince of peace not only helps me discover my errors, but also brings me peace. I work out ways to make amends; hurt feelings are healed, and I experience greater growth in life. So when you feel the need to say something, do so with God's guidance, and with God our mistakes become opportunities to grow.

## Let's Pray Together

**Heavenly Father,**

There is never a time that we need you than right now. We are complexed and confused of when to speak and not to speak. But, Lord, we want to enter into your presence. We want to be in a place where You meet us. Guide us to that place. Lord, forgive us for being careless and unthinking in the way we approach You. Your Word says, "Blessed are the pure in heart, for they shall see God" (Matt. 5:8). We thank you for the confidence and the strength you have given us. We acknowledge that You are a holy and righteous God. Thank you for the privilege of being able to enter with confidence into the place where You dwell, because of the atonement that Your Son has made on our behalf. Teach us that we must follow Your instructions and ways if we want to remain in your presence. We pray this in the name of Jesus, the Lamb of God who takes away allour sin. Amen.

# Poem # 5
## ( A Weeping World )

*A weeping world is not fun to see*
*People hurting, crying, and confused,*
*Having no one to hold their hands or wipe their tears*
*Jesus is standing with arms wide open saying this is for you.*

*Christians, when your way seems darkest,*
*When your eyes with tears are dim,*
*Go to God your Father quickly*
*Tell your troubles all to him.*

*In this world, Lord teach me how to love and work*
*So that everything I do,*
*May bring love and peace through you to my brother*
*A service good and true.*

*This weeping world has lost its foundation*
*And everything is in an uproar,*
*We say that we are Christians*
*But no one hears Christ as he knocks at life's door.*

*A gem can't be polished without friction*
*Nor can we be perfected without trials,*
*Holding on to the cares of this weeping world*
*Takes away every moment beautiful smile.*

*It has lost focus of its creator*
*No more love, joy, and happens at all,*
*It's people are lost and out of control*
*Everybody is reluctant and having a ball.*

*For a world that is falling out of control*
*No one seems to care,*

*But without the love of Christ*
*It is soon to fall in despair.*

*When things are out of hands*
*God has someone to handle the hills and curves,*
*We as Christians are here to help*
*This old weeping world.*

# Chapter Four

## Facing Danger That Surrounds Us

" Yea, though I walk through the valley of the shadow of death, I will fear no evil: for thou art with me; thy rod and thy staff they comfort me." Psalms 23:4

Nothing keeps you more on the alert than knowing you are in the line of fire meaning you are facing danger each and every day. It doesn't matter whether you are at home, riding to work in your car, or at work; danger is around. Facing the danger that surrounds you on a daily basis can and be stressful. Psalms 91:3-6 (NIV) states: "Surely He will save you from the fowler's snare and from the deadly pestilence. He will cover you with His feathers, and under His wings you will find refuge; His faithfulness will be your shield and rampart. You will not fear the terror of night, nor the arrow that flies by day, nor the pestilence that stalks in darkness, nor the plague that destroys at midday.

When my Army National Guard unit and I were deployed in Iraq in support of Operation Iraqi Freedom: at times it brought a lot of fear to the mind of many in my unit. As I talk with many of them, they all had different concerns and worries to deal with. All of which had arrived from the fact that we were here in an hostile environment where the enemy desires to sift us as wheat. The most difficult reason to fear the danger around us is that we are fighting an enemy we can't see. When facing danger that surrounds us, we can't help but to give thanks to the Almighty God at all times. Psalm 91:7-8, (NIV) states: "A thousand at your right hand, but it will not come near you. You will only observe with your eyes and see the punishment of the wicked." It's not because you're so good that you are kept by God when danger surrounds you, but it's because you are His child and He loves you and therefore He makes ways out of no way so that you are covered by His promise. By His wisdom the Lord laid the earth's foundations, and by His understanding He also set the heavens in place. So with our finite minds, we cannot comprehend the mind of Christ and what He intends to do with and for us. So as we go day by day here in this hostile environment, we can be assured that our foot will not stumble, and when we lie down, we will not be afraid. In knowing this when we lie down, our sleep will be sweet.

Regardless of the planes being shot down, buildings being blown up, roadside bombs exploding, and suicide car bombing we are still covered under the blood of Jesus. I can remember the night we arrived in the country of Iraq we didn't know what to expect or what we were actually here to do. The feeling and thoughts of being ambushed and maybe losing our lives plagued a lot of us as we tried to sleep. We would stay close around one another and talk and encourage one another that everything will be alright. We sang praises to God thanking Him for His grace and mercy and His perfect love, as we keep telling ourselves that no weapon formed against us shall prosper. We may endure for a night but joy is going to come in the morning. Those sleepless nights were the nights that we were to endure so that God's joy could come in the morning. The apostle Paul stated, "Finally, be strong in the Lord and in His mighty power. Put on the full armor of God so that you can take your stand against the devil's schemes. For our struggle is not against flesh and blood, but against the rulers, against the authorities, against the powers of this dark world and against the spiritual forces of evil in the heavenly realms. In situations like these, when you are facing danger on every side you can't be to careful. As we live from day to day we see that this century and this world has weapons that can kill thousands of people at one time. Different countries uses different technologies such as chemical weapons or nuclear warfare which can literally destroy a whole city, but the thing I like is despite the magnitude of the disaster the weapons could cause, God has promised us we can stand in the midst of it untouched! Clearly, when God says, "a thousand may fall at your side;" He's not talking about heaven. God is talking about a place here on earth where you're seeing lots of disastrous things happen to the wicked all around you, and yet you are totally protected unharmed. He let us know that we are covered by an invisible shield, a secret place that the world knows nothing about. What we have to realize is that when we are in that place, it doesn't matter how terrible the situation might be, you can make it through in safety. The situation may look bad and seem like you have taken all you can handle, you must hold on to God's most holy word. "For in the time of trouble He shall hide me in His pavilion: in the secret of His tabernacle shall He hid me; He shall set me up on a rock. Psalm 27:5, kjv. This further lets me know that even in this midst of bullets flying, mortar rounds exploding, missiles being shot, and roadside bombs being detonated, we are hid from our enemy and resides under God's protection. I can attest to these situations from experience. While being deployed here in the country of Iraq we've encountered some close calls. Some of us were shot at as we travel from one camp to the next, some have been attacked by roadside bombs, and some of us have had close encounters with mortar attacks. This showed us that we were covered by God's love like a mother eagle covers her babies by spreading her feathers over them. The devil couldn't get to us because His love was our shield and buckler.

My awareness of God's love is like my experience with door closers. I needed him to protect me from all hurt harm and danger. This personal touch was there because in the same way, God's love is all around us, even if we don't notice. The most comforting thing about God is we see signs of his love everyday when we maintain a personal connection with him through our relationship with Christ. God knows when our minds and hearts are filled with the noise brought on by illness, stress, fear, or pain. Though God is always near, sometimes being still can help us to recognize and experience God's presence. God's repeated call for individuals and nations to be still is recorded in the bible. As we take a look when Jesus used the phrases be still it encourages us to hold on, and believe we are in his care even with the danger that surrounds us. " He woke up and rebuked the wind, and said to the sea, 'Peace! Be Still!' then the wind ceased, and there was a dead calm. " ( Mark 4:39 )God sometimes calls to us in gentle, comforting words. At other times God shouts to get our attention, but always God speaks in love, as parents seek to comfort their children. " Be still," God says. " Leave your worries with me and know that you are loved." I remember the first night we heard mortal fire, my first thought was, I am going to die! I felt totally alone and Helpless. Although I was afraid, I continued to trust God. This incident reminded me of how we all respond to God when we are in a crisis. We feel alone and become so afraid that we panic and think we will not survive, but this is not true; God has promise to be with us and take care of us, no matter what the outcome may be. All that we need has been prepared for us by God. If we do not panic, we can remember what we have been taught and He will not let us drown in our crisis. In times of crisis, stop and listen for God's voice, that's his promise of protection when you are surrounded by danger.

## Let's Pray Together

**Heavenly Father,**

Paul prayed in 2 Thessalonians 1:11, "That our God may count you worthy of his calling, and that by his power he may fulfill every good purpose of yours and every act promoted by your faith." We ask you to count us worthy of your calling and to enable us to fulfill Your purposes, through the grace, faith, and authority we have in Christ. Thank you for never giving up on us but for redeeming us for Yourself and Your purposes through Jesus Christ, the Second Adam. And forgive us for spending more time dwelling on our own plans, ideas, scenarios, analyses, and schemes than on taking Your Word to us and let us rely on you alone. We pray this in the name of Jesus, who is the Living Word. Amen.

# Poem # 6
## ( Traveling With No Vision )

*Traveling with no vision*
*Is like a car without wheels,*
*You just watch it*
*In the yard or driveway sitting still.*

*With no vision the people perish*
*They have no lead, nor light,*
*It's like they are in the darkness*
*Fighting with all their might.*

*Some say I think I have one*
*Some say I don't,*
*But think about it*
*The truth is they are not sure what they want.*

*The cure to this weakness*
*Is easy to see,*
*Just remember to call on Jesus*
*And weep at His feet.*

*As we travel from place to place*
*We still can't find rest,*
*Because we've taking our eyes off Jesus*
*And forgotten that he is the best.*

*Visions happens to prove*
*The work that Christ has assured,*
*For all of his followers*
*To both witness and concur.*

*I know at times it seems strange*
*And sometimes unclear,*

*But trusting in Christ*
*Should be 365 days a year.*

*So to end I must say*
*To travel with no vision,*
*Is like running a stop sign*
*You must make a decision.*

# Chapter Five

## Listening For That
## Silent Whisper

I know the first question that arises in your mind is; what does a silent whisper have to do with God's protection in the midst of danger? My friend, though you are saved and serving the most high and holy God, at some point or another you are going to stop and listen for His silent whisper as He speaks to you. One thing we have to realize is that we have angels at work for us and they will safely keep us. "For He shall give His angel charge over thee, to keep thee in all thy ways. They shall bear thee up in their hands, lest thou dash thy foot against a stone." Psalm 91:11-12, kjvIn the Middle East during the summer it was very hot, and when you was there during a military operation, there was certain equipment that you must wear at all times. In addition to wearing all this gear you may have to perform missions all day long and when this happens you don't have time to study or read God's word the way you would like. So what happens is you have God's angels that encamps around you to catch you and deliver you from the struggles of the day. They encourage you to hold on and listen, which means to isolate yourself from everything else that's going on around you and hear God speak to you if it is only one or two words.

This is a still small voice that lingers with us and it speaks to us even when we don't want to hear. When it speaks no one knows where it came from nor where it is going; but deep down on the inside we know it is far more different than anything else that we have experienced before. What is so strange about this still small voice is that is gives you hope. While working, while studying, while having fun this little whisper will only be heard when you take time to listen to what it is trying to say to you. Just as the wind blows and no one knows which way it blows, this still small voice is a mirror image of how deep God's love is for us to depend on. At times we pretend that we are too busy to hear or answer the call, but turning a deaf ear to God's call is only putting ourselves in the arm of the deceiver. How wonderful this must be to have a friend in Jesus to care about you, your love ones, and those around you when all else seems to be going wrong. Romans 8:28, "Let us know that all things work together for the good of them that loves him and that are called according to His purpose, and it also ensures us that it can be a soft pillow for a tired heart."

In reality we must accept that Jesus died for us and He takes care of us no matter what. His love is never ending and He longs to give everyone an opportunity to witness this amazing experience for themselves to have that motivated speech when telling about this joy. Once the importance of this experience has reached the hearts of all of us then we can truly say that God is good all the time and all the time God is good. The silent whisper gives you the assurance that God is on your side and He cares about every moment of your life even when you are asleep and not knowing that you are here on this earth. This is why the psalmist said, "that he will bless the Lord at all times and his praises shall continuously be in His mouth, because great is the Lord and greatly to be praised." So as we journey through this life there will be times when we only here those things that sounds good and what we want to. God is still there to lead the way with His grace and mercy to help keep us from falling out of His will and not easily giving into the enemy which is our deceiver. His love is never ending and this is why we should continue to give Him the praise, the glory, and the honor that is due to Him.

"For every battle of the warrior is with confused noise, and garments rolled in blood; but this shall be with burning and fuel of fire. For unto as a child is born, unto us a son is given: and the government shall be upon His shoulder; and His name shall be called wonderful, counselor, the mighty God, the everlasting Father, the Prince of Peace." Isaiah 9:5-6, kjvWe should always be assured that God will never turn His back on His children. His word is true all by itself and He don't need you to add to nor take away to try to make it of none affect. When He speaks to us it is for our own good and we need to obey Him, not only because He's God, but because of the fear we have of doing wrong in His eyes.

He is so patient with us that He gives us chances after chances to get it right before Him, so sooner or later we will hit life's end if we don't turn and listen to that silent whisper that calls our names when we are going through and suffering for His name sake. Just remember as long as you are here and a servant of God, you are going to have to sit idle sometimes to hear this voice of the whisperer. There is one other thing that you can depend on and that is His love is deeper than any other.

## Let's Pray Together

**Heavenly Father,**

Like Jesus disciples, we too, need to be taught and learn how to trust your words. We have to be sensitive to the spirit to hear what it is saying to us. You have called us to a lifestyle of prayer, and we ask You to fulfill that calling in us. Give us a heart to seek an intimate relationship with You every day and to follow Your thoughts and ways rather than our own thoughts and ways or other's opinions. We pray that You help us to spend more time in prayer so we can hear You when You speak to us in that still small voice. We also pray that we will place our trust in You and Your Word rather than in words of faith all around us that are contrary to Your truth. We pray this in the name of Jesus, our Great Intercessor. Amen

# Poem # 7
## ( Why Let The Devil Win )

In the beginning God created the heaven and the earth
And the earth was without form,
And knowing that God spoke earthly things into existence
Is the reason I'm writing this poem.

When you're on the battle fields for the lord
Witnessing, praying, and helping to save souls,
Don't let the devil win
Remember that God is in control.

As I sit and think on all the things my heavenly father has created,
The stars, the sun, the moon, the grass,
The flowers, the water, you, me and the land
There's no way I'll give my life to the devil and his evil hand.

Creation was spoken into existence with such devasting powers;
So get behind me satan you low down dirty coward.

Everything God made was good from the beginning
And nothing was left undone,
So why let the devil win and keep you on the run.

Why let the devil win
And not even put up a fight,
When your heavenly father has assured you
That everything will be alright.

Why let the devil win
And keep you in despair,
When you have a heavenly father
That sits high and sees all from the air.

*Why let the devil win*
*And treat you like you are his own;*
*When God has promised he'll never forsake you nor leave you alone.*

*Why let the devil win*
*When we know he's full of deceit,*
*It's like living a life without Jesus*
*You're never complete.*

*As you sit and listen to these encouraging words*
*let's not forget what you have heard;*
*As time goes by and we're reaching an end*
*Don't give up ask yourself WHY LET THE DEVIL WIN?*

# Chapter Six

## Being Content To Do Our Part

We are sure to have God's promise of protection around us at all times, but we must not forget to do our part. I want to remind you that receiving that protection is conditional for each individual, it's a personal thing. You have to know what God has said before that shield and buckler will work for you. As a child of God, you have to hear it from God's word and receive it for yourself saying, "That's mine, deliverance from God belongs to me!" You must assure yourself that whatever God promise you, it is yours just for being obedient. As we journey through our Bible we can see the promises that God had promised to His followers and how every one of them was fulfilled. Now for you and I today God has left for us a promise and if we are willing and obedient we can benefit from this promise and eat the good of the land. We must make Him and His word as a vital part of our daily routine and believe in Him to protect us no matter what, but to do this we must do our part. As sinners, we must admit that we are sinners in order to be reconciled to Christ. Following, we must accept and believe what His word has challenged us to do. Once we accept this change and have prayed a prayer asking God for forgiveness of all our sins, and to restore unto us His salvation in believing that He is the son of God, and that He was the one that rose the third day with all power in His hands. It is then that God began to work in our behalf and give us the benefits of serving a true and living God. And in doing our part we must allow God to work for us, trusting that He will take care of His own and make everything alright. We must also continue to pray, fast, and study God's word to keep us alert of the devil and all of his tricky ways. Therefore, since we have been justified through faith, we have peace through our Lord, Jesus Christ; through whom we have gained access by faith into this grace in which we now stand. You see, at just the right time, when we were still powerless and unbelieving, Christ our Lord and Savior died for the ungodly. I thank God for Jesus, because now we have a right to the tree of life because of Him dying and shedding His own blood for our sins.

As a soldier, serving here in the country of Iraq, it wasn't very easy. I had to constantly remind myself that God has not given me the spirit of fear, but of love, power, and of a sound mind. This had to be one of my main key verses to myself, especially being a minister of the gospel and sharing it with God's people daily. There were times when not only the troops felt like giving up, but I did to. Thanks be to God that we over came with the help of God and we were able to get through each day. As I carefully sit down and consider all that Jesus did, His selflessness, sacrifice, servant hood, humility, and patience were all out of love for us and concern for our eternal destination. Christ was obedient to the point of dying on the cross so that we could experience eternal life. Knowing that when He was on the cross, we were on His mind. That is enough to convince me to do my part.

One thing that burden some Christians is when all else fails, we forget about the instructions we have read. We are often so eager to get started on something new or another ideal that we ignore the perfect instructions that were provided to us. Our impatient nature doesn't allow for such inconveniences! But when we get stuck in the middle of a trial or project we wonder why. When we do finally look at the instructions, we find the important step we have missed. God has provided us a guidebook for faithful living. It helps us to stay focus on doing our part as we should. Why then, do we continue to frustrate ourselves by attempting to figure out life's uncertainties and mysteries on our own?

God has blessed us with wisdom and knowledge to bless them who are in dying need of a savior. And because God loves us and wants to help us, God has given us the wisdom found in the scripture to guide us as we face new projects and trials each day. As saints we ain nothing by waiting until all else fails before immersing ourselves in God's instructions. One thing is for sure and through prayer and meditation and reading Gods' word, we find help with the troubles, projects, and let downs of our lives and avoid many of life problems. Prayer: Lord

I know that I am not all that I can be, but help me to consider your ways. Thank you, lord, for providing the bible for ou instruction. And lord, if nothing else, help us to follow its guidance faithfully, in Christ's name. Amen.

Now just before we do any type of cardio exercise during the day, week, or month we do these stretching exercises. As we do these stretches using our legs, arms, and toes we may feel twinges of pain and discomfort up and down our arms and legs as we do the stretches to stretch the muscles. We do these exercises to increase blood flow and to help prevent injuries to our muscles, tendons, and ligament, but also to increase the flexibility of our muscles and allow a wider range of movement. Just as we need to stretch our muscles to increase their range of movement, so do we need to stretch our capacity for Christian love. Our capacity to love is increased when we stretch to love those we may find hard to love: Those who are enemies, those who have hurt us deeply, those whom we disagree with, and those who are very different from us. Being content to do our part is nothing more than being Christ like. It is called spiritual longsuffering to be Christ like, and to be a follower of Jesus Christ is to love in a way that is constantly stretching us and expanding us beyond boundaries and limitations. Can we grow and mature enough in our faith to emulate the boundless flexibility of the heart of God? I say yes we can, but we have to be content to do our part firstLet's

## Pray Together

**Heavenly Father,**

Your Word says, "Be self-controlled and aware. Your enemy the devil prowls around like a roaring lion looking for someone to devour. Resist him, standing strong in the faith" (1Peter 5:8-9). Let Your Holy Spirit show us where we are being deceived in our attitudes toward prayer and the Word so we can understand and practice true and effective prayer. We ask You to help us remain alert to the hurdles in our lives that the enemy wants to use to destroy our prayer potential. Lord, don't allow us to walk away from Your truths and forget them. Help us to study these principles and consider carefully Your ways as revealed in Your Word. Then encourage us to step out in faith to put these principles into practice in our lives. As we do, we thank you for answering our prayers and doing immeasurably more than all we ask or imagine, according to Your power that is at work within us. We pray this in the name of Jesus, who resisted the enemy through the power of Your Word. Amen.

# Poem # 8

## ( You Are Never Alone )

*Jesus shares your worries and cares*
*You'll never be left alone,*
*For he stands besides you to comfort and guide you*
*He always look out for his own.*

*If you know Jesus in all of his ways*
*You'll never walk alone,*
*To be tempted of the devil and his tricks*
*Keeps you assured that one day your going home.*

*Why do we keep on trying*
*The fare of this world's sin,*
*When God has set before us*
*The joy of Christ within.*

*We understands that grief will not last*
*For through our tears we clearly see,*
*That while we part but for a time*
*With Christ we'll spend eternity.*

*You will never be alone*
*Christ has assured us this in His promise,*
*So hold on to His word*
*Until He returns at His second coming.*

*Lord, help us to love the way that you love*
*The humble, the lowly, the meek,*
*And help us to care the way that you care*
*For sinners, the outcasts, and the weak.*

*So when you're feeling alone and unworthy*
*And wish for a kind, loving friend,*

*Remember that God longs to show you*
*A love that never will end.*

*The times of our path is rough and steep*
*Our way is hard to see and hope is gone,*
*This is when we ask, Why is life unfair*
*Jesus then answers, follow me you're never alone.*

# Chapter Seven

## Dealing With The Stress
## And Lack of Support

One thing that plaque the troops early on in the war, Operation Iraqi Freedom, was the stress with lack of support. Stress is a very powerful symptom to deal with especially in the time of war and being away from love ones, family and friends. Stress causes sickness and some soldiers were hampered by stress and committed suicide, suffering severe headaches, and even high blood pressure. Stress will cause your body to shut down and not function the way it is suppose to due to lack of support from your bodily organs. Like everything else when bodily organs start to not function properly, it affects something else and causes the stress level to increase. We as soldiers really had to depend on one another and watch one another, because the odds were against us. We would be in 100 to 130 degree heat, almost all day and nothing is going right. At times not enough water, and at night we could not sleep because it was too hot. Due to the extreme heat, as we slept during the night, there will be balls of sweat running down your neck and legs. It was most frustrated because over in Iraq is a lot of camel spiders and they will crawl everywhere. So during the night you will hear screaming and yelling from soldiers sleeping quarters because of the sweat thinking that a spider was on them.

Not only dealing with this brought on a lot of stress, but the fact of getting bit by sand flies, and mosquitoes that you didn't have any control over. These insects will bite you and leave bumps on your legs and arms that will itch you for days. So to beat the stress of dealing with these bites, you will have to be done with all you had to do and in bed covered with your mosquito net before dark. Out in an environment like this, makes one really miss the comfort of his or her bedroom. So just when we thought it was bad it got worse, there were no bathrooms or any showers to use for cleanliness. To operate around these issues there were soldiers in the unit who built portable showers. In the bathroom, they also built a portable stall to use and we burned the waste once a day.

To leave home to come to something like this was never expected, but as we came and learned we knew something had to be done to accommodate the troops. Life here in Baghdad isn't easy dealing with the things of life as you would have back home. Not only as soldiers, we were dealing with mental and physical stress and a lack of support. As soldiers we didn't have a stable supply chain that could get us parts, equipment, and the clothing we needed. It was too hard trying to continue driving unsafe humvees up and down the streets of Baghdad. It seems like a plan that was not thoroughly implemented and because of the situation, we continued to suffer with stress. It was hard leaving home and to come and fight a war not knowing what to expect, and most of all not getting the support you needed. It was by God's grace that we have made it as far as we have, due to the fact that the enemy had already plan an ambush for our lives. During many missions and/ or escorts that we were tasked to do, Satan had his plan already in place to take out some of the soldiers from 1166thMilitary Police Company, but still today I'm very thankful that the hand of the Lord was upon us and still is unto this very moment. Everyone doesn't know what it feels like to be sheltered and locked in and no freedom on your behalf at all. It is like being behind bars at a state prison facility and somebody is always giving orders for some detail that needs to be completed.

Even though we are tasked with convoy escorts and missions, we didn't know anything about where or what we were going to do, all we had to lean on was the word of the Lord that "No weapon formed against us shall prosper," it won't work. Also, being that the support and stress levels were swinging out of control we knew that it was time Lord to do something before the enemy comes in and causes trouble in the camp. This is when we accepted the word of God for what it really means from Psalm 91:14-15 N.V. "Because He loves me," says the Lord, "I will rescue him; I will protect him, for he acknowledges My name. He will call upon Me, and I will answer him; I will be with him in trouble, I will deliver him and honor him." Accepting these words of the Lord was like loading up all the weapons we had and was for sure that we could take on anything that would get in our way. Regardless of our stress level and lack of support, as soldiers in the army of the Lord, we had to stand firm on God's word to defeat Satan and his tricks.

Our biggest obstacle was getting to know who Satan really is and the problems he has and can cause. Satan is the enemy of God. He wants to destroy everything God has created. He is also called the devil, the evil one, the prince of this world, and the god of this age. Satan brought this evil into the world, and he lies, destroys, and attacks the people of God. It was great to know that Jesus came into the world to renew what Satan had destroyed. Satan tried to stop Jesus, but Jesus is God's son, and he has more power than Satan. Yes times were more stressful than others, but we had to endure the hope of our joy which was in our Lord and savior Jesus Christ. Oftentimes, we experience some hindrances and pressure from the outside world as well as our very own loved ones. It occurred to me later that from time to time I needed to see what interrupts my contact with God. Sometimes there are big issues involved that make talking to God in prayer very difficult. But far more often it is seemingly trivial things that ruin my communication with God. The memory of an irritating moment, the thought of an item I'd overlooked in shopping, or the key I had mislaid. It is then I have to remember the advice that if something is worth praying about, however trivial it may seem. When I realize how disruptive these hindrances can be, I can deal with them first, clearing the way for more disciplined prayer and a deeper relationship with God.

Even though we were in a hostile environment I knew that our only answer to this situation was to put it all in God's hand. When faced with reality first hand the only thing or the best thing to do is ask the Lord to help us to deal faithfully and patiently with the small things that can distract us from a relationship with him. One thing that threaten us the most is the act or prejudice of other, but if we would just let the iron curtain fall we will be able to see that people are not as bad as they seem. Propaganda is awful indeed! So is prejudice, but they are not new. We see them even in the Bible; consider Jacob, from the book of Genesis. For years Jacob was convinced that his brother Esau was an enemy who wished him dead. Jacob could not imagine that Esau might have changed. When he was reunited with his brother, Jacob realized that he had no reason to be scared. Esau had become a totally different person. We may have prejudice about people. We may think they are always the same and cannot change. We may be so sure in our opinion of others that we won't give them a chance to change. This can hinder us in our relationships. People do change, as the statement earlier affirms it is possible, but we cannot know they have changed unless we approach them.

Then we can see if our opinions and attitudes are out dated and need to be changed. So to deal with these types of issues, and concerns do not make it any easier to deal with the matter of stress you encounter along with lack of support. Like the scripture in Ephesians 4:23 states, " Be made new in the attitude of your minds." And the apostle Peter stated it plainlywhen he said, "Like good stewards of the manifold grace of God, serve one another with whatever gift each you have received." In dealing with the stress and lack of support, we've learned to depend on God's unchanging hand no matter what's the case or situation.

## Let's Pray Together

**Heavenly Father,**

Your Word says, "Let us throw off (lay aside) everything that hinders and the sin that so easily entangles, and let us run with perseverance the race marked out for us" (Hebrews 12:1). Let us not worry about the trouble that surrounds us, but let us stay focus on Your Word. As Your Word says; we are burdened by things that hinder us spiritually and emotionally, and we too easily become entangled with sin. These encumbrances keep us from having a joyful, unbroken relationship with You and with our families, friends, coworkers, and others. We ask You to enable us to have a true understanding of who we are in Your Son, Jesus Christ. We ask that You help us to forget those things that are behind us and press toward that higher calling which is in Christ Jesus. Help us to clear away each of the hindrances in our lives so we can live freely of Your will and purposes for the world. We ask this in the name of Jesus, who is our Burden –Bearer and who has carried our sins and sorrows, who has healed us by His own wounds, and whose suffering on our behalf has brought us peace with You. Amen.

# Poem # 9
# ( The Great Turnaround )

*The lord will turn your life around*
*If you'll invite him in;*
*Then you'll at once be heaven bound,*
*No longer chained by sin.*

*If you can't forgive those*
*For the wrong they have done to you,*
*Go to them and talk it over*
*That's the Christian thing to do.*

*Lord, I've not always understood*
*What plan you have for me;*
*Yet I will glory in your cross*
*And bear mine patiently.*

*I pray that when I sense your call to serve,*
*Help me to follow through;*
*I must not just stand by and pray*
*When there is work to do.*

*When many began to follow*
*Some make it and some don't,*
*They will run the race swiftly*
*But by the end they will be in want.*

*It's not about your pride*
*Or how much pain you could bare,*
*It's about that great turnaround*
*And knowing Jesus is always there.*

*He loves to hold you*
*Inside of his loving arms,*

*To share his glory*
*And spread his loving charm.*

*So, Lord help us to value the freedom*
*Of life we receive from your love,*
*A life of obedience and service*
*Kept safe by your hand from above.*

# Chapter Eight

## After Having Done All
## To Stand, Still Stand

When you look back at where God has brought you from and what He has done in your life, through it all you still stand. If you just take a look at some of the people of God in the bible days, that no matter what; they stood still in God's word. Because of their faith in God and what He is capable of doing, they were able to stand the tests that came upon them. Take for instance, Noah, when he was instructed by God to build an ark. He didn't fight what God instructed; instead he sat, listened, and began to gather materials to start building. Because of Noah's faith, he was for sure what he was doing was for a just cause. Not let's journey back and think on this situation. Noah was instructed to build an ark to prepare for a flood, but what was so ironic is, it had never rained on the earth at all. For Noah it was a step of faith believing God that in order to survive the flood, he needed an ark built to the specification given by the Lord himself. Not only did He tell Noah how to build it, but He also told him what to build it out of. "I am going to bring flood waters on the earth to destroy all life under heavens, every creature that has a breath of life in it. Everything on earth will perish." Genesis 6:17, N.V.

I can imagine that while Noah was building the ark; as he was instructed by God, the people as they walked past was making fun of what he was doing. Calling him names, saying he is foolish for making something that big. Noah trusting in God as he did, did not pay his enemy any attention. He was believing God, for God had promised him that he was going to establish His covenant with him, that he and his wife, sons and son's wives will enter in. Through Noah, not only was his wife, sons and son's wives were saved; but two of every living creature, male and female was too.

The Lord then said to Noah, "Go into this ark, you and your whole family, because I have found you righteous in this generation. Take with you seven of every kind of clean animal; a male and it's mate, and two of every unclean animal; a male and it's mate and also seven of every kind of bird, male and female; to keep their various kinds alive throughout the earth. Seven days from now, I will send rain on the earth for forty days and forty nights, and I will wipe from the face of the earth every living creature I have made." And Noah did all that the Lord commanded him. Genesis 7:1-5, N.V. Through Noah's obedience, we can learn that there is safety in trusting God.

Now let's take a look at Daniel and his act of obedience before the Lord, and how his faith stood the test of time for him. Daniel was faithful, and he was faithful in hisservice to the king and to his god, but the officials who were trying to get Daniel fired had to try and trick him to choose between God and the king. At this point the officials were jealous of Daniel because Daniel was one of the three presidents of the empire, second only to the king himself. The officials being who they are, suggested that the king pass a law that would forbid anyone from making petition (or praying) to anyone other than the king himself for thirty days. It was also suggested that whoever broke the law would be thrown into a den of lions. So when the king read this petition, his ego was touched and he immediately signed the law on the spot, not thinking what it would mean to His administrator Daniel.

Now when Daniel learned that the decree had been published, he went home to his upstairs room where the windows opened towards Jerusalem. Three times a day, he got down on his knees and prayed, giving thanks to his God, just as he had done before, Daniel 6:10, N.V. Daniel knew about the kings new law, but he didn't change his routine of prayer, he just kept praying. After it was all reported to the king about Daniel's behavior, it grieved the king, he trusted Daniel and respected him. The king didn't want to throw Daniel into the lion's den, but he had been tricked. So the king gave order, and they brought Daniel and threw him in the lion's den. The king said to Daniel, "may your God who you serve continually, rescue you!" Daniel 6:16, N.V.

Here we notice what the king said to Daniel, he told him to serve God continually. Daniel was an abider, and he was faithful. He stayed constantly in the presence of God and service of God, and because of his faithfulness, God delivered him.

Let's take a look at three more men of God. Shadrach, Meshach, and Abednego who was also on a king's staff. They were Hebrews who had been captured, but God's blessing was upon them in such a degree that they had been given great responsibility over the affairs of Babylon. Being that they served and trusted God, they to like Daniel, had a decree issued to them from the king. Despite the king's decree, they refused to bow down to the king's image. Being under such pressure from the king, the three Hebrew boys had made up in their minds that if God is for me, who can be against me. They were so dependable upon God that the king ordered to have them thrown into the fiery furnace to be burned. After commanding his strongest soldiers in his army to tie up Shadrach, Meshach and Abednago; he also ordered that the furnace be heated seven times hotter. Not realizing that his tactics were not going to work as he had planned, "The king command was so urgent and the furnace so hot, that the flames of the fire killed the soldiers who put up Shadrach, Meshach and Abednago in the furnace." Daniel 3:22, N.V.

After seeing the test of the Hebrew boys, king Nebuchadnezzar with the right attitude couldn't help but to give God the praise. Again, it was the stand of Shadrach, Meshach and Abednago, that delivered them.

Last of all, one of my favorites was Joseph. Joseph was a young man, seventeen years old, out in the field tending his fathers flock. Now because Joseph was born to his father at an old age, he loved him more than any of the other brothers. Because of his love, he made Joseph a richly ornamented robe and when his brothers saw that their father loved him, the more they hated him. Joseph being a young teenager at the time did not notice the change in his brothers' attitude, he just kept on tending his fathers flock. One day while out in the fields, Joseph had a dream and he told his brothers' and they hated him even more. He told them that they were out binding sheaves of grain out in the field when suddenly his sheaf rose and stood above theirs and their sheaves gathered about his and bowed down to it. His brothers said to him, "Do you intend to reign over us? Will you actually rule us?"And they hated him all the more because of his dream and what he had said.

Now Joseph had yet another dream in which he insisted that his brothers' hear him. He told them that his dream showed the sun and moon and eleven stars bowing down to him. This time Joseph felt that it was important that he let his father know about this one. When he told his father, as well as his brothers', his father rebuked him and said, "what is this dream you had? Will your mother and I and your brothers actually come and bow down to the ground before you?" Genesis 37:10, N.V. Even though Joseph couldn't see what was happening around him, he was still determined to do his fathers will. Joseph was determined that the dreams he was having were true and nothing could make him doubt them.

Joseph's life can be summed up as a flock attendant at age seventeen, a dreamer sold into slavery by his brothers', sold to Potiphar and became his attendant, put in charge of his household and Potiphar entrusted Joseph to his care, and everything he owned. From here, Joseph was put in prison by Potiphar where the king's prisoners were confined. Now Joseph was placed in charge of all those held in prison and all that was done there. Joseph's life now has reached the point where he is now interpreting dreams. After interpreting dreams, Joseph was blessed and put in charge of the whole land of Egypt. At age thirty, we can see that Joseph had to endure ups and downs, trials and tribulations for thirteen years before climaxing to the point where God was trying to get him. This is why we should clearly see what the apostle Paul was saying when he said, "After having done all, still stand."

So, being a soldier deployed here in Baghdad, Iraq; I had to learn the hard way of having done all you can, still stand. There were times when myself and other soldiers would just spend hours calling on the Lord and even though we didn't see any results right away, we kept on praying. Now it is eleven months later and we are still here in Iraq, but nevertheless, we were still marching strong; the trumpet is about to sound and we will be marching to a different sound. Soon and very soon, we will be headed back home to reunite with family and friends, the pain and suffering of loneliness will all be over, so again I thank God for blessing us and keeping us as well as He has, because there were times when we all just felt like giving up. Better yet, I thank God for helping us to maintain selfesteem. Although the times were rough and we didn't quite understand all that was happening; to me what might seem hard to understand, was the way we felt about ourselves and the dependency on our appearance or abilities. If you believe that you don't have what it takes to win at life, you are apt to confirm your own prediction. So by contrast, good self-esteem is a blessing. There are going to be times when it seems like all else fails, but holding on to God's promise will not leave you hopeless nor disappointed. Some of us are still struggling with self-esteem, but the difference is the hope we feel in our savior. We choke on our pride. It wells up in our throat and we want to fight, to swear, to yell, to cry when we feel wronged by another. But now we can say instead, thank you lord. I praise you for sending your grace, mercy, and your word. I know that all things work together for good to those who love God. We can stand assure that it is working. Lately the lord has taken what started out to be terrible days for us and turned them completely around so that we feel a warm, loving glow within, and I am smiling and thinking of others rather than ourselves.

We oftentimes wonder where can we began? It has been said that the best way to get rid of an enemy is to make him your friend. This is true of the things that seem to threaten your image in God. They can be the means by whichyou discover your real purpose, power, and potential. How do we make these enemies our friends? Let them do for you what self-confidence, self-satisfaction could never do. Let your weakness push you to dependence on God. He alone can give you an ever lasting reason to feel good about yourself. Don't be afraid, or if you are, let your fear bring you to the one who loves you. The results of acknowledging that you have been on the wrong path will far outweigh any temporary pain of confession. You will soon find great relief as a result of admitting to God that you have sinned against him by banking on the world's values. Romans 3:23 says, " For all have sinned and fallen short of the glory of God." So then, we as saints, must confess Jesus Christ as our designer, our Lord, and our Savior. Trust Him to save us on the basis of the payment for sin he made on the cross. Accept the fact that when He died, He died for us all when he rose from the dead, he rose to make his life available to all who would believe. This is the first step to a new beginning and understanding how you can stand even after you have done all to stand. It is God's answer for a new birth, a new identity, and a new potential. It's found in the one loves us more then we could ever love or care for ourselves. Again, to all who read this novel, in any given situation, After having done all to stand, still stand; and bless the name of the Lord.

## Let's Pray Together

**Heavenly Father,**

You have taught us that when we pray, we are to bring others' needs with us. Fasting is a form of intercession, and we want to be empowered by Your Spirit through fasting so we can minister to others and counteract the work of the enemy. We consecrate ourselves to You in prayer and fasting, setting ourselves apart to seek You and Your will, rather than our own interests. Jesus said if we ask for anything in His name, You will do it (John 16:23). We know that we cannot ask in Jesus' name unless we ask what is according to Your will. There is no other name by which we make our requests but the name of Jesus. We call on the power of His name to meet all our needs. You have said that those who hear the Word and receive it, those who allow it to sink into their hearts, are like good soil (Matt. 13:23). Yet the power is in the Word. It is the Word that will bring forth good fruit in us and spring up within us to everlasting life. Lord, give us the confidence that if You said it, You will do it; if You promised it, it will come to pass. Thank You for Your Word. Thank You for the faith that you have given us. Help us to expect a miracle. We pray this in the name of Jesus, our High Priest, who sits at Your right hand and intercedes for us. Amen.

# Poem # 10
## (Why not age gracefully)

Why not age gracefully
It is no harm to you,
Just remember the will of God
And it will keep you looking anew.

The wrinkles on a time - worn face
Can be symbols of God's grace,
If through our laughter and our tears
His love has freed us from our fears.

When you let God's love fill your heart
It will show on your face,
So during this aging process
Just thank him for his amazing grace.

We cannot fully know God 's greatness
His wisdom, power, and care;
But it's enough to know
That he is with us everywhere.

Time may wrinkle the skin
Worry, doubt, hate,and the lost of ideas wrinkle the soul;
One key attribute is a lifelong faith in God
Who assures he would carry you even when you're old

In this aging process, help us to redeem the time
You give us everyday,
To take each opportunity
To follow you and obey.

Lord teach us to number our days
That we may gain a heart of wisdom,
To make the most of our earthly existence
With the love you have given through your freedom.

*As we age from day to day*
*There is much to do faithfully,*
*We could take Gods' word at heart*
*And not worry about aging gracefully.*

Thank You Lord For Deliverance
Thank You Lord Thank You Lord
Thank You Lord